ALL THE BUILDINGS* IN NEW YORK

*THAT I'VE DRAWN SO FAR

BY JAMES GULLIVER HANCOCK

UNIVERSE

INTRODUCTION

JAMES GULLIVER HANCOCK

I grew up in Sydney, Australia, with open spaces, going to the beach every day, burning my feet on the sand, with the scent of jasmine blooming on every corner. So New York was a shock—a good kind of shock but a shock nonetheless. Like most Australians, I've traveled a lot and lived in many different places. I've traveled from Australia to England, via the Trans-Siberian Express (though it wasn't much of an express). I've lived in Paris, Vienna, Berlin, London, Los Angeles, Montreal, and Indonesia. Also, like most Australians, I have heritage in different places around the world, and struggle to define a sense of "home."

During all this traveling, I was fascinated by the details that made each place unique—the small ephemeral things, the daily objects and habits that made places different from one another. I began to feel that a place was defined by small everyday differences rather than large ones. What made them home was not the language or tourist attractions or landmarks—

it was the everyday things. Indonesia was unique in how they lay concrete. London was unique in how the buildings joined the pavement. Japan was unique in how the tiles were laid.

It is this fascination—"an obsession," if you will—with everyday details that helped me to understand my place throughout my travels. This has led me to naively attempt to document "All the rooftops in Paris," "All the cars in Los Angeles," "All the snow in Montreal," "All the rain in London," and "All the bicycles in Berlin," among others. When I finally made my way to New York, the greatest city in the world, this idea took on a new intensity.

Newcomers to New York City really want to own it, to make up for all the years they've missed living here. My way of doing that was drawing my surroundings, so I could become more involved and connected with my new home. Many visitors come to this city and fall in love with it. What I fell in love with was the density of experience here. This is a chaotic, awkward, historic, and organic

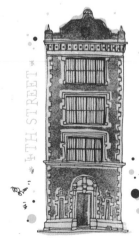

city organized on a grid. Although perfect buildings, like the Chrysler Building or the Statue of Liberty, symbolize "I Love NY," it is the other ordinary buildings, spilling with hectic daily life, that hold real New York life and passion. The fact that they stand right next to the icons is what makes this city special.

This collection and obsession have become an almost ritualistic undertaking, a therapy of sorts, helping me to organize the overwhelming infinity and chaos of New York into something I can know and understand. Sometimes it appears to me like the game Tetris; the buildings begin to fit together neatly and become familiar. At other times it seems like an unquantifiable mess. This diarylike process helps me to deal with the waxing and waning, from complete chaos to intimate detail that is New York, making it personal, one object at a time.

It's odd how familiar everything seemed when I arrived in New York City. Probably because growing up, I was exposed to a range of American clichés through television and movies, and my earliest and most romantic visual associations are with New York. When I first moved here, I lived in Brooklyn, on a street that looked exactly like Sesame Street. I half expected to find Oscar the Grouch in one of the trash cans. And it wasn't only Sesame Street. Other neighborhoods drew further associations: *West Side Story* in the Upper West Side, *Rear Window* in Greenwich Village, *Breakfast at Tiffany's*

on Fifth Avenue, *Ghostbusters* in the beautiful buildings around Central Park, *Do the Right Thing* in Bed-Stuy, *Manhattan* in . . . Manhattan—the list goes on. I felt as if I knew everything about the city—the fire escapes, the fire hydrants, the subway, the way the streets are cleaned—but all from a screenplay, from certain camera angles. So it wasn't a real understanding, and I didn't feel connected to the reality behind the "film set" that I was walking around in.

So I started this project, "All the Buildings in New York," as a way to help me connect to my new city and to overcome these clichés. My natural state is to draw, so I devised an ingenious plan to draw the most complicated thing I could see around me: all the buildings, with all the details, all the windows, all the chimneys, all the pipes, and even all the spiderwebs between the pipes. I am remapping this magnificent city for myself, outside of the clichés, one building at a time. Now I find myself running into the buildings I've drawn and greeting them like old friends.

Drawing is my way of understanding the things around me; it's how I get comfortable and intimate with them. This project has made me friends with New York, and I hope it does the same for you. It is a guidebook of sorts, helping you to see new details and characters within the city. This is an ongoing project; follow the journey online at www.allthebuildingsinnewyork.com.

COMPLETED IN 1812
DESIGNED BY
JOSEPH-FRANÇOIS MANGIN
&
JOHN McCOMB Jr.

OLDEST CITY HALL IN THE U.S.A.
STILL BEING USED FOR GOVERNMENT
FUNCTIONS LIKE THE MAYOR'S OFFICE

CITY HALL

GOTHIC REVIVAL STYLE

CONSTRUCTION COST
$13·5 MILLION.
FRANK WOOLWORTH
PAID IT
IN CASH

233
BROADWAY
WOOLWORTH
BUILDING

COMPLETED IN 1913
DESIGNED BY CASS GILBERT

TALLEST BUILDING
IN THE WORLD FROM 1913–1930!

792 FEET!

1 WALL STREET COURT

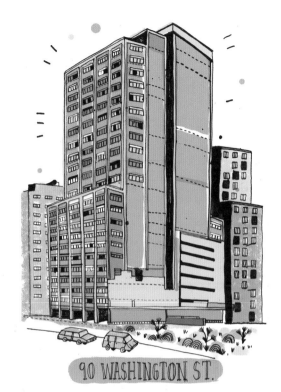

90 WASHINGTON ST.

1 WEST STREET

75 WALL STREET

200
WEST
STREET

62 BEACH STREET

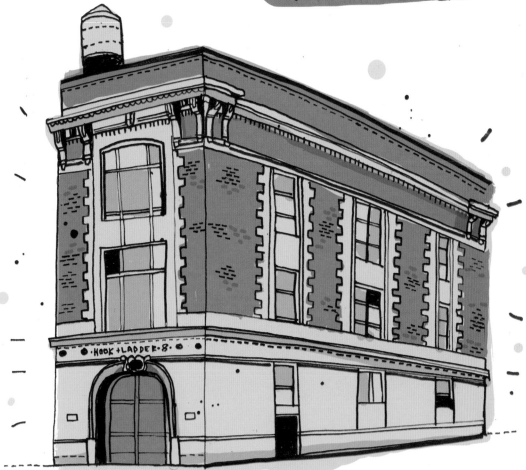

HOOK + LADDER · 8 ·

14 NORTH MOORE ST.

HOOK & LADDER 8
(WHERE THEY FILMED GHOSTBUSTERS!)

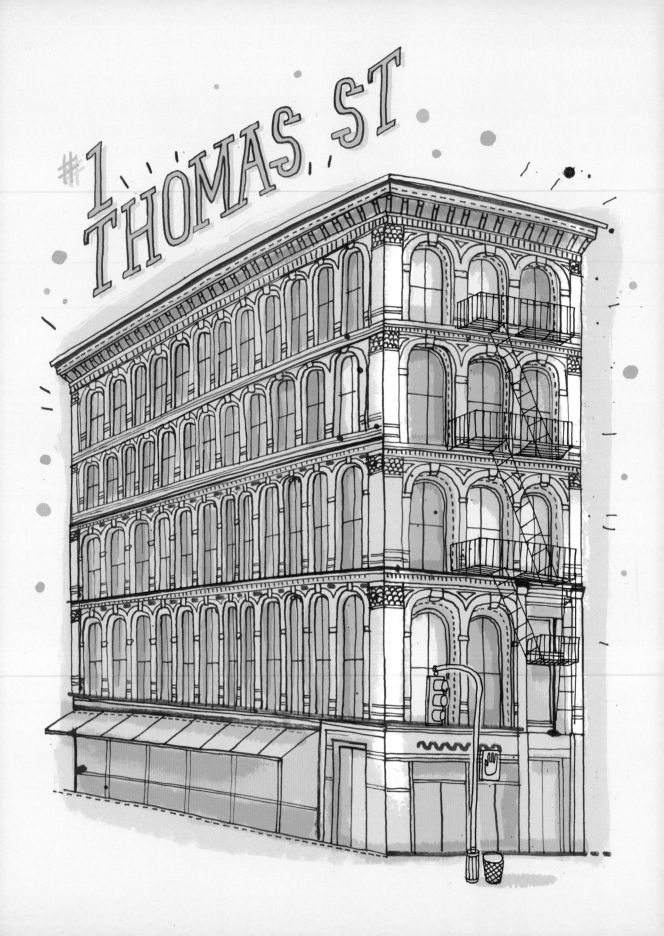

83 MOTT ST

CHURCH OF THE
MOST PRECIOUS BLOOD
109 MULBERRY ST

THE LIBRARY

STANTON ST

ORCHARD ST.

RIVINGTON ST

LUDLOW STREET

210 LAFAYETTE ST

PUCK BUILDING
295 LAFAYETTE ST.

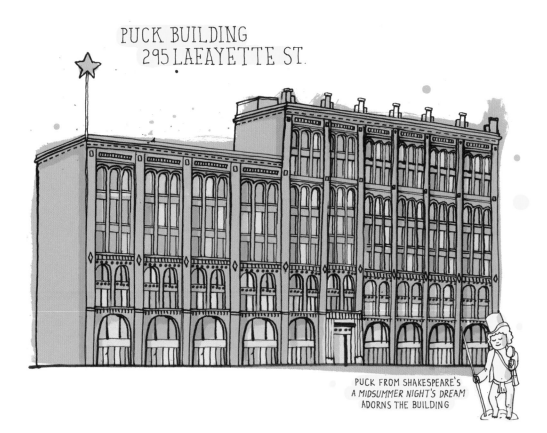

PUCK FROM SHAKESPEARE'S
A MIDSUMMER NIGHT'S DREAM
ADORNS THE BUILDING

22 MERCER STREET

136 BAXTER ST

58 CHARLES ST

75½ BEDFORD ST

147 WAVERLY PLACE

794 BLEECKER ST.

77 PERRY STREET

120 GREENWICH STREET

45 HORATIO STREET

1 MORTON SQUARE

THE EXTERIOR OF

THE COSBY HOUSE

10 ST. LUKE'S PLACE

(BUT IN TV LAND THIS HOUSE WAS IN BROOKLYN)

56 JANE ST

55 WEST 8th. STREET

8 EAST 8th. STREET

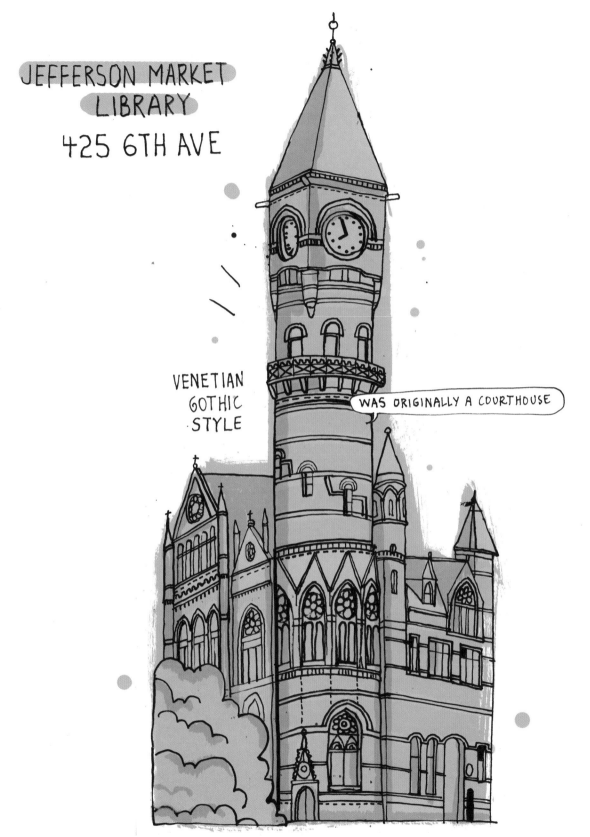

WASHINGTON SQUARE ARCH

MADE FROM MARBLE

during excavation a coffin was found 10 feet under here

CELEBRATES THE CENTENARY OF GEORGE WASHINGTON BECOMING PRESIDENT.

385 6th AVENUE

WASHINGTON MEWS

142 WEST 4TH ST

70 UNIVERSITY PLACE

9 St. MARK'S PLACE

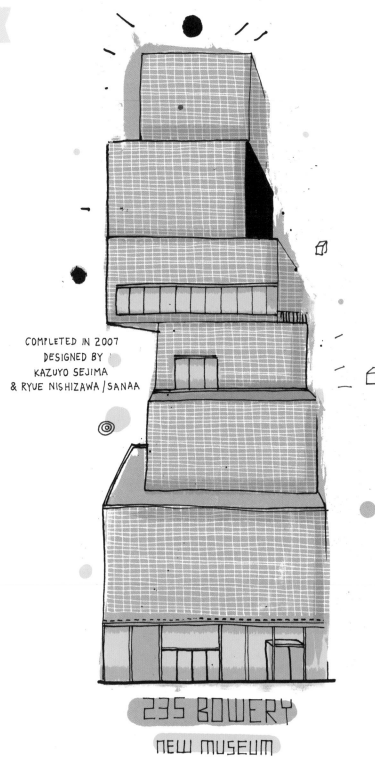

COMPLETED IN 2007
DESIGNED BY
KAZUYO SEJIMA
& RYUE NISHIZAWA / SANAA

235 BOWERY

NEW MUSEUM

107 AVENUE C

121 EAST 23RD STREET

110 5th AVENUE

FLATIRON DISTRICT

170 5TH AVE

7 EAST 20TH STREET

301 EAST 22ND STREET

FLATIRON
BUILDING

(NAMED SO BECAUSE
IT IS SHAPED LIKE
AN OLD FLATIRON)

ORIGINALLY NAMED
THE FULLER BUILDING

COMPLETED IN 1902
DESIGNED BY DANIEL H. BURNHAM

JACK KEROUAC WROTE *ON THE ROAD* HERE

WAS HOME TO:

BOB DYLAN, CHARLES BUKOWSKI,
JANIS JOPLIN, LEONARD COHEN,
IGGY POP, DYLAN THOMAS,
ANDY WARHOL, ALLEN GINSBERG,
GORE VIDAL, STANLEY KUBRICK,
JANE FONDA, JIMI HENDRIX,
MADONNA, FRIDA KAHLO ETC ETC.

HOTEL CHELSEA
222 WEST 23RD ST

CHELSEA

GOOGLE
76 9TH AVE

ONE OF NEW YORK'S MOST ENERGY EFFICIENT SKYSCRAPERS

New York Times BUILDING

COMPLETED IN 2007
DESIGNED BY RENZO PIANO

ST PATRICK'S CATHEDRAL

COMPLETED IN 1913
DESIGNED BY REED & STERN
AND
WARREN & WHITMORE

GRAND CENTRAL TERMINAL

AKA "GRAND CENTRAL STATION"

IT WAS THE WORLD'S TALLEST BUILDING FOR 11 MONTHS BEFORE IT WAS SURPASSED BY THE EMPIRE STATE BUILDING

AN ART-DECO CLASSIC

COMPLETED IN 1930 DESIGNED BY WILLIAM VAN ALEN

THE CHRYSLER BUILDING

8th Ave. @ 55th St.

PARK

211 EAST 53RD STREET

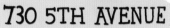
46th St

730 5TH AVENUE

61 WEST 62ND STREET

ROCKEFELLER CENTER

HOME TO
30 ROCKEFELLER PLAZA
(30 ROCK)
& RADIO CITY MUSIC HALL

THE TOP IS ILLUMINATED DIFFERENT COLORS TO MATCH THE SEASON

OBSERVATION DECK ON THE 86TH FLOOR

THE EMPIRE STATE BUILDING

YOU CAN ALWAYS FIND YOUR WAY BY LOOKING FOR THE EMPIRE STATE BUILDING

THE PLAZA

1 CENTRAL PARK SOUTH

25 SUTTON PLACE

767 5TH AVE

THE UNITED NATIONS

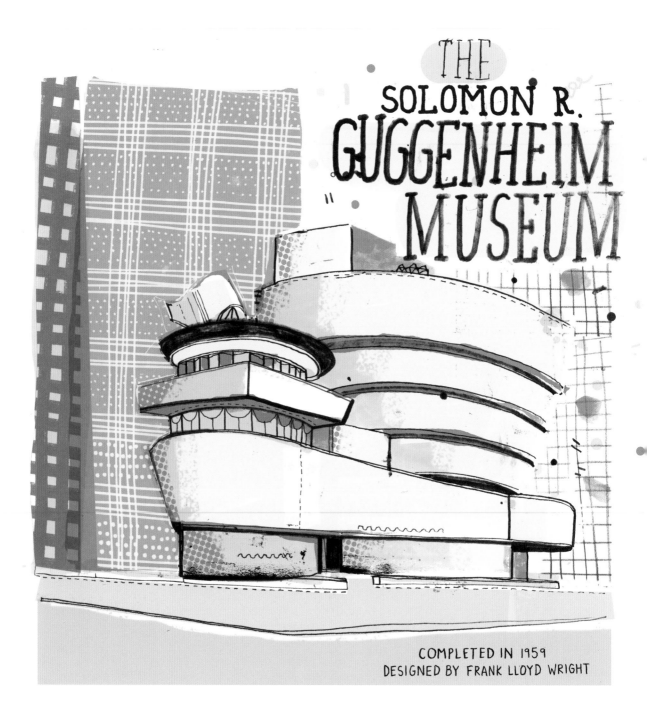

THE
SOLOMON R.
GUGGENHEIM
MUSEUM

COMPLETED IN 1959
DESIGNED BY FRANK LLOYD WRIGHT

180 EASTEND AVE

8 EAST 83RD ST.

360 EAST 88TH ST.

450 EAST 83RD ST.

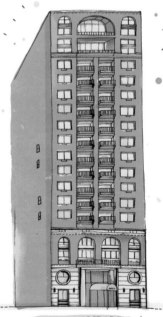

LE CHAMBORD
350 EAST 72ND ST

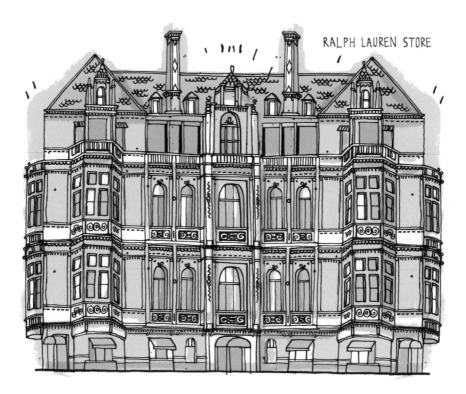

RALPH LAUREN STORE

888 MADISON AVE

1045
**PARK
AVE**

PARK AVE   EAST 86TH ST

301 EAST 75TH ST

COMPLETED IN 1966
DESIGNED BY MARCEL BREUER

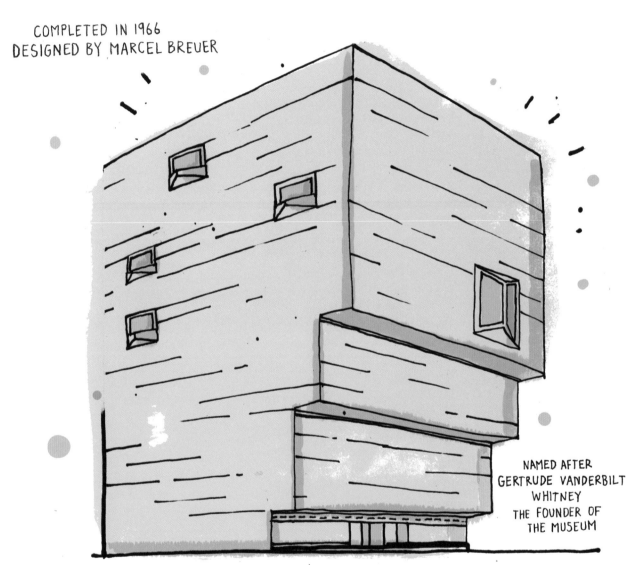

NAMED AFTER
GERTRUDE VANDERBILT
WHITNEY
THE FOUNDER OF
THE MUSEUM

THE WHITNEY

MUSEUM OF AMERICAN ART
945 MADISON AVE.

A TAXI TO

THE METROPOLITAN MUSEUM OF ART

THE LARGEST ART MUSEUM IN THE U.S.A. CONTAINING OVER 2 MILLION WORKS

SINCE OPENING IN 1880 IT HAS GROWN TO 20 TIMES THE SIZE

340 WEST 86TH ST.

71ST + BROADWAY

MARYMOUNT

LINCOLN CENTER

FOR THE PERFORMING ARTS

HOME TO THE AVERY FISHER HALL,
THE METROPOLITAN OPERA HOUSE,
AND DAVID H. KOCH THEATER

145-146 CENTRAL PARK WEST

150 COLUMBUS AVE.

320 CENTRAL PARK WEST

25 CENTRAL PARK WEST

AMERICAN MUSEUM
OF NATURAL HISTORY

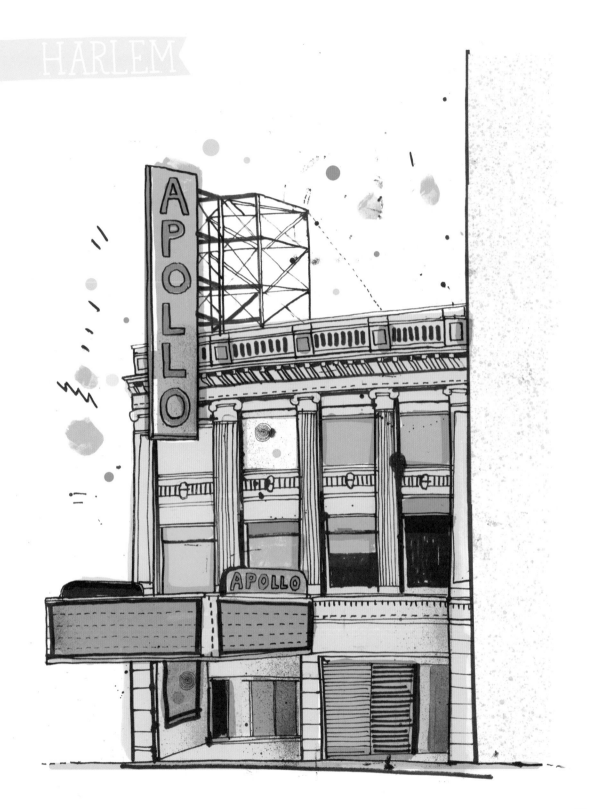

ENID A. HAUPT
CONSERVATORY

AT THE
NEW
YORK
BOTANICAL
GARDEN

58

161-164 GRAND CONCOURSE

618 EAST 138TH ST.

QUEENSBOROUGH
BRIDGE

P.S.1

QUEENS

G FROM
GREENPOINT

PRIMARY SCHOOL #1
NOW AN ANNEX TO M.O.M.A.

ONE OF THE OLDEST SUSPENSION BRIDGES IN THE U.S.A.

BROOKLYN BRIDGE

DESIGNED BY JOHN AUGUSTUS ROEBLING
COMPLETED BY HIS SON IN 1883

BROWNSTONES ON SOUTH PORTLAND ST

THERE ARE MANY BROWNSTONES IN NEW YORK CITY, ESPECIALLY IN BROOKLYN NEIGHBORHOODS SUCH AS PARK SLOPE, CLINTON HILL, FORT GREENE, COBBLE HILL, AND BROOKLYN HEIGHTS. THEY ARE ELEGANT ROW HOUSES FACED WITH A REDDISH-BROWN SANDSTONE (ALSO CALLED BROWNSTONE), BUILT FROM AROUND THE 1840s → 1900.

CONEY ISLAND

Thanks to my family, Lenka and Quinn, and to everyone who have supported this project thus far,
including Town Real Estate. Thanks also to Gloria Nantz and all at Rizzoli.
And thanks to my dad for giving me $50 at the airport on my first overseas journey.

Designed by Susi Oberhelman

First published in the United States of America in 2013 by
UNIVERSE PUBLISHING
A Division of Rizzoli International Publications, Inc. • 300 Park Avenue South • New York, NY 10010 • www.rizzoliusa.com

2013 2014 2015 2016 / 10 9 8 7 6 5 4

ISBN: 978-0-7893-2467-2 • Library of Congress Control Number: 2012941048 • Printed in China